MW01502554

WIFE
SCHOOL

(Every Husband's Best Friend)

"The man who finds a wife, finds a treasure"
(Proverbs 18:22).

Mrs. B. J. Fountain
(Wil Fountain's Good Thing)

Wife School
Every Husband's Best Friend
B. J. Fountain

Published By:
KPG Book Publishers
(a division of Kingdom Publishing Group, Inc.)
P.O. Box 3273, Richmond, VA 23228
www.kingdompublishing.org

Library of Congress
© 2011 by B. J. Fountain

ISBN: 978-0-9848940-6-2

Cover design: John Price

Printed in the United States of America.

To My Husband, Wil

You are a just man and my best friend. I love you and I respect the man of God that you are and that you are becoming.

Thank you for not being afraid or intimidated by my addictive love for God, my call to the ministry, my three children and my strong leadership ability.

I appreciate your prayers and support in heading our household and your partnership in ministry. I could never personally reward you, but I'll keep trying. I know there are rewards in Heaven for your deeds of love.

I honor you for being an example to our sons and daughters of how a husband should love his wife and how a Godly father heads his home, works hard and makes his family a priority.

You have one of the biggest hearts I have ever seen. I admire your love for children, single moms, and the elderly. You're always serving others even when you don't feel well.

What on earth did I do to receive such a gift from God as you? Only a loving Heavenly Father could create and send someone as incredible as you into my life. He uses you to bring out the best in me.

We are, and will always be an awesome dream team. I love being your wife. The best is yet to come.

When this book hits the bestseller list (and it will), I am buying you the fishing boat of your dreams.

With All My Love,

Your Extraordinary Wife for Life
—BJ

❖ INTRODUCTION ❖

My name is Bettie Jean Fountain, but you may call me B. J. I have enjoyed being the extraordinary wife of Wil Fountain, Sr. for more than twenty years. According to Wil, I am "a great wife."

In high school while my peers were busy planning for college and lifelong careers, I was scorned because my only aspiration at that time was to be a Godly wife and mother.

Out of my desire to be a wife and mother, I married my childhood sweetheart at 17 years old, four months before my high school graduation. To this union came two beautiful daughters and a fine son (there is not a thing wrong with him).

Little did I know that having a wedding didn't automatically make me a real wife any more than having children made me a great mother. It didn't take me very long to realize I knew practically nothing about being a wife and even less about being a good mother.

I had embarked upon a journey that presented extremely difficult challenges that I was not prepared mentally, emotionally, spiritually or financially to handle.

Could someone have prepared me for the 10 plus years of heartache and pain, the guilt and shame, disappointment, broken promises and countless unmet expectations and dark days? Where did I go wrong?

With much thought, prayer and spiritual counsel, this wife knew she and her children were destined for greater things. So, in the best interest of all concerned she let go of her little girls' fantasy world and walked toward the reality of the good future she believed God had prepared for her.

All the glory belongs to God, and special thanks to the late, Bettie Wallace (the greatest mother who ever lived), to my family and church friends for their love, support and well intended advice during and after my stormy years that led to yet another painful divorce.

Many times she thought, "I wish I knew then, what I know now." Things would have been a lot different.

Well, guess what? This ever-learning, ever-growing and ever-changing wife has gained a wealth of valuable life lessons through the past two decades. She is now ready and willing to share with the world her wisdom treasury from a wife whose life is devoted to God and to her husband forever.

After over twenty years, one of my greatest joys in life is being Mrs. B. J. Fountain—Wil Fountain's good thing from God. I am a voice to women of my generation and generations to come.

I have a testimony that nothing is impossible with God. After two divorces in the church, I am now a forgiven, loved, healed, whole, joyful, submitted wife for life.

This is Wife School 101. Let's get started....

TABLE OF CONTENTS

1

WELCOME TO WIFE SCHOOL

Hello, beautiful women of the world, welcome to Wife School 101.

On Memorial Day, May 30, 2011, God changed my life. That's the day Wife School (which is soon to be a best selling book) was birthed in my spirit.

Recently I have been thinking a lot about how close I am getting to retirement age. It became clear to me how unprepared I am for the kind of retirement life I have envisioned. I diligently began to plan and research career and education options, and decided to pursue a degreed nursing program.

For the past several months I have tremendously enjoyed working for a home health care agency as a Certified Personal Assistant. Since my job is not always demanding it allows me time to read, study and research while taking good care of my patient and finishing all my daily assignments efficiently.

I decided on a nursing degree program, ordered my transcripts and begin a diligent study of my nursing assistant manual. I felt this would familiarize me with basic nursing techniques and medical terminology before starting the general education courses.

On this particular day while studying my nursing book, I heard in my spirit, "He that finds a wife finds a good thing and obtains the favor of the Lord" (Proverbs 18:22). I began to write what I thought would be a verse or two or a few thoughts on the last page of my notebook.

As I continued to study I heard the verse again, he that finds a wife, with the emphasis on "he finds a wife" ... Not a girlfriend, not a baby mama, a wife....

◆ He That Finds a WIFE ◆

NOT A

LAZY, CRAZY, UNORGANIZED, INDECISIVE, ARROGENT, BITTER, INSECURE, FEARFUL, GOLD-DIGGING, IMMATURE, WHINING, MOODY, PITIFUL, WEAK, ANGRY, UNFORGIVING, MEAN-SPIRITED, SELFISH, IMPATIENT, IMMORAL, UNTRUSTING, SELF-HATING, UNSURE, EXCUSE-MAKING, UNPOLISHED, WOUNDED, BLEEDING, EMOTIONALLY NEEDY, PAIN-IN-THE-BUTT, BLOOD-SUCKING HELLION!

HE IS SEEKING A WIFE—
A HELPER SUITABLE FOR HIM FROM GOD!

◆ Proverbs 18:22 ◆

KING JAMES VERSION

Whoso findeth a wife findeth a good thing, and obtaineth favour of the LORD.

NEW LIVING TRANSLATION

The man who finds a wife finds a treasure, and he receives favor from the Lord.

THE MESSAGE

Find a good spouse, you find a good life—and even more: the favor of God.

AMPLIFIED BIBLE

He who finds a [true] wife finds a good thing and obtains favor from the Lord.

CONTEMPORARY ENGLISH VERSION

A man's greatest treasure is his wife—she is a gift from the LORD.

NEW CENTURY VERSION

When a man finds a wife, he finds something good. It shows that the Lord is pleased with him.

YOUNG'S LITERAL TRANSLATION

[Whoso] hath found a wife hath found good, And bringeth out good-will from Jehovah.

I remember thinking, "Lord, I know this. I am already a wife, I have been a wife since February 1991. I have been found."

I heard the words "WIFE SCHOOL."

Soon, like a river all these thoughts of what a True Wife/Real Wife is began to flood my mind. I heard things like "you were already a wife. You did not become a wife on your wedding day." I smirked and thought, "He was just a 'he' until he found me."

I made my initial notes on the back page of what I had intended to be my nursing notebook and resumed my study of medical terms. Soon, I begin to hear again, "A True Wife—A Real Wife." I begin writing from the back of my notebook toward the front. I quickly had 3 pages, 5 pages, 10 pages full of writing about this extraordinary wife for life. Finally, I realized that not only a book, but a new dimension of ministry was being birthed.

Today I would like to share with you a small portion of what I believe with all my heart I heard from God to help the women of the world who have resolved to be Godly wives.

I believe a true wife will be sought out from among all the other women of the world by her husband.

I believe every Godly woman has the potential to be an exceptional wife.

I believe I did not become a wife on my wedding day. I was already a wife, hidden treasure waiting to be found by my husband.

✦ Suggested Reading ✦
Genesis 2:18–20

The Hebrew Word "ezer" is translated "help meet" in Genesis 2:18-20 (KJV). Ezer: Help MEET, helper suitable, "ezer kenegdo", companion, counterpart, comparable, fit, just right, etc...

Other Bible translations include:

"helper suitable" (NIV, TNIV, NASB)
"a helper comparable to him" (NKJV)
"a helper, a companion... a suitable companion" (the Message)
"a helper fit for him." (ESV)
"a suitable partner for him." (CEV)
"an helper—as his counterpart." (YLT)

"a helper who is like him." (HCSB)

"a helper meet (suitable, adapted, complementary) for him." (Amp)

"a helper who is just right for him." (NLT)

Do you hear the Father? A true wife is a helper....

Yes, I do realize that many Christians, church folks, religious spirits, other groups and entities will disagree with me on some or all of contents of this book. That is a risk I am willing to take.

I believe that God have given me as a Voice to the wives, and anyone else with a teachable spirit. Lives will be changed for His Glory.

To everyone reading this book, please understand me, hear my heart. Before learning the true meaning of a wife, my bad attitude toward God and men had to be dealt with. I literally said to God, "if this is all you got to offer, you can keep them (referring to men). I want nothing to do with Your boys." Still deep inside me, I wanted to know, "Where the hell are all the good men?"

◆ 2 ◆

WHERE IN HELL ARE
ALL THE GOOD MEN?

A question no one could answer to my satisfaction but Father God, Himself.

My beloved sisters, the hardest lesson I had to learn was to kill the bad attitudes toward men. My mind had to be renewed regarding men in general before becoming a suitable helper for my husband.

Picture this, I grew up among the daughters without dads in the home and spent no quality time with him. My precious mother struggled, yet successfully raised six of her seven children. We were active members of a small church where the Pastor was a strong woman and very few men attended. The old neighborhoods growing up were mostly women and children. The few men visible were known adulterers, drunks, workaholics, perverts, criminals, wife abusers and you name it. I spent a lot of my childhood and youth fighting off horny neighborhood boys and men, close relatives included. Needless to say, my perception of men was not a good one. So just like some of you, I was left wondering, "where the hell are all the good men?"

Even as I am writing this book, Father is teaching me. He just said within me, "Those men you just related to did not know Me. None of them were your husband. You were not their good thing. Forgive them and move forward."

One of my favorite sayings just came to mind: "All you know is all you know."

I said all that to say this: a true wife, unmarried or married, has ceased ALL negative thoughts, remarks and attitudes toward men and is actively encouraging her family and peers to do the same. Daughters, sisters, nieces, cousins, girl friends, we must all unlearn such remarks as:

"I just want to know where in hell all the good men are?"

"I'll never get married because ..."

"Always a bridesmaid, never a ..."

"I can do bad all by myself"

"I have given up on all men ..."

"All the good men are ..."

"All men are dogs"

"All men think about is ..."

Darlings, it's a new day, and you must renew your mind. Radically change your thinking about what it means to be a Godly wife. Instead of saying "All men are dogs," say "All men were created in the image and likeness of God. So within every man is the potential to be like the Father." Join with me and other devoted wives in praying for our husbands and all men instead of cursing them. We did this in the past when we didn't know the power of life and death was in our mouth.

It is always right to kill (cast out) any attitude that demeans another human being, especially men, and especially if you want a good husband. Think before you speak. If all men are dogs, then why do you want to marry one and what does that make you?

Now back to the answer of where the good men are. Some say all the good men are in prison or dead or unborn. I say, all the good unmarried Godly men are presently seeking the Kingdom of God, and His Spirit is leading each of them in his search for a wife—a suitable, adapted, complementary helper for him."

Now pay close attention, all you unmarried, separated, divorced or wives in transition, and be sure it is a husband you are desiring, and not a Father Figure, an Enabler, a Room Mate, a Sugar Daddy or a Baby Daddy.

✦ 3 ✦

YOUR HUSBAND IS NOT
YOUR FATHER

According to the *American Heritage Dictionary*, a father figure is an older man, often one in a position of power or influence, who elicits the emotions usually reserved for a father.

From my personal experience and that of other women I know, it seems common for a woman who did not grow up with her dad (and some who did) to be attracted to older men, and many times these men who are very similar to their daddy. This could be part of the reason a lot of girls fall for their pastor, a deacon, a teacher, a boss, or another authoritative figure.

I encourage you ladies (and men), when necessary and if possible, please reconcile broken relationships with your daddy, the sooner the better. I was 28 years old before having the first conversation with my daddy. It was very awkward, but necessary for me. I remained silently angry with him for many years until I realized my anger at him not only affected how I related to God as my Heavenly Father, but also how I related to men in general. Being able to verbalize my forgiveness to him helped greatly with my healing process.

This is how my journey to thorough forgiveness and progressive healing took place with my dad. If you are helped by this or anything else in my book, please e-mail wifeschool@verizon.net. Your comments would be greatly appreciated.

Now, back to my daddy experience. I begin to pray for him often, whether I felt like it or not. I would only call him on happy days. Happy days are those holidays that begin with "Happy" and "Merry." A typical example is, "Hi dad, this is your daughter B. J., I just called to wish you a Happy Birthday before going off to work, hope you have a great one. Okay, bye-bye now." Get the concept? Now, if you don't do holidays, you could try, "Hi dad, this is B. J., just wanted you to know I was thinking about you and hope you have a good day." Just do it. Courage isn't the absence of fear. It is the ability to do something needful even when you feel afraid. Have you picked up the phone yet? Don't make me come over there.

My advice to you when making this difficult call is, always talk to Father first, ask for courage and wisdom. You can do this alone or with a friend. You could also have a close friend or your spouse hold your hand during the call. One other suggestion, which is one I highly recommend, is to play soft music in the background. I have found this to be very helpful to me. A personal favorite of mine is Juanita Bynum's, "You Are My Peace," instrumental. Soaking Music is great as well. Still not ready? Then, send a note or letter or simply write him a letter in your journal/diary. Make an effort and trust the outcome to the Lord. I believe if you will do the possible, God will do the impossible.

Daughters without dads, remember this, whenever you do anything toward honoring your earthly father with a clean heart and pure motives, you have all of Heaven aiding you. Sweetheart, own this statement, you are not responsible for your dad's response to your love. It may be favorable and it may not be, but there is one thing I do know, "Love never fails."

Beautiful daughters, I extend to you right now a big hug from the Father above and within. Receive it now. Um, I just received mine too.

Okay, back to my daddy story. As best as I can remember, one of the hardest things I ever did regarding my daddy was finding him the perfect Fathers' Day card. (By the way, there is a great untapped market out there for you card writers. I may even give it try myself if I ever finish this book.)

This is all so funny right now, but it was not funny on that day. I was sweating profusely while proceeding to read one card after another. Finally I picked a card. On the outside it simply read "Happy Father's Day, I love you." The inside of the card was blank. Well, at least half of the mission was complete. I had purchased him a card.

So there I was at home, sitting and starring at this blank Father's Day card for what seemed like forever. Finally, I prayed, "Lord, what in Heaven's name do I write in this card? I don't even know who he is, what he likes or dislikes, his favorite color or food. I can't think of one good thing about him. Not one thing. Father, You created him, You know him. Please tell me one good thing about him. I heard the answer within ... "YOU." You are one good thing about him. He is the one I used to bring you into this world." My tears and Father God's words began to flow like a river. In no time at all I had filled that card with heartfelt loving words from my Heavenly Daddy to my earthly daddy, letting him know how much he was loved by His Creator and by his daughter. This was one of the most life-changing, liberating experiences in my life. This same God who did this for me, can do this and even greater for you. Ask Him.

In a way that only a loving Heavenly Father could, He assured me I was loved by my daddy and that he had done the best that he could based on his upbringing and his lack of spiritual knowledge. I wish I could tell you that our father-daughter relationship blossomed after that. Another one of my favorite sayings is: "Tell yourself the truth."

The truth is I still think of him and pray for him often and I always will. This is my way to honor him. I still call him on happy days with soft background music most of the time. I confess that I am strong in the Lord, but while taking that Fathers' Day card to my dad I was sweating and shaking like a leaf, but I knew I was doing the right thing (honoring my father). The Father's Day visit went well. He did all the talking, and here I was worried about what I would say. I got to see him from a whole new perspective. Now I know where my siblings and I got our sense of humor, and a lot of our facial expressions.

Upon recently visiting him at the hospital I got to meet one of my brothers from another mother. How divine.

Ladies, renew your mind, your husband is not your father. He can never replace your absent father.

All I can truly say from all of this is, God is real, forgiveness is powerful. And ladies, *do* deal with your daddy issues, preferably before becoming a wife, or at least begin the process as soon as you finish reading this book. Promise me you will do this. Okay? Let me know how it goes. Contact me if I can help in any way.

Being a wife doesn't mean you stop growing spiritually. You don't give complete control of your life to another. That's enabling....

4

AN ENABLER
IS NOT A HUSBAND

Make sure you want a husband and not an enabler. Being a spouse
involves a continual dying to self. A true wife can handle her
husband's honesty when she is acting outside of the character of
Christ. Marriage is about iron sharpening iron.

My definition of an enabler, for the sake of this book and as it
relates to a wife, is a man who can be manipulated and controlled—
one who is afraid to tell you the truth, especially about your obvious
destructive behavior.

Since this is Wife School, may I add that I have seen many
women who seem to marry men they can control, and then become
highly upset when they don't make good husbands and leaders in
the home, and can't live up their warped expectations. Please, forgive
me if that statement seemed harsh.

Yes, I do realize that there are as many men as women who
need to be taught God's principles for marriage, but at this appointed time my assignment from my heavenly Father is to help
prepare the unmarried women to be Godly wives, and to empower
the married women to enjoy their roles as wives devoted to God.
Keep in mind, I am talking about real husbands here (not mere
men, those born males) according to the standard of God's Word,

not the world's standard. We have to get back to Our Father's original plan in everything.

Some unhealthy behavior patterns an enabler may allow from you may be one or more of these:

Drinking too much

Spending too much

Overdrawing bank accounts/bouncing checks

Gambling too much

In trouble with loan sharks/check cashing agencies

Working too much/not enough

Maxing out the credit cards

Abusing drugs (prescription or street drugs)

Getting arrested (bailing you out)

Physical/verbal abuse

Any of a number of other unhealthy behaviors/patterns of addiction.

The *Urban Dictionary* definition of an Enabler:

> Supports another's bad or dangerous habits by staying silent or by providing assistance such as money, transportation, approval, etc.

Enablers tend to fear calling others out on their destructive habits because these "others" tend to be friends, family or people close to the enabler. Rather than risk losing the love, respect, friendship or contact with the person, the enabler chooses instead to play it safe and watch the other slowly destroy themselves or others through their own actions.

A real wife will not substitute an enabler for a husband.

Let's keep it moving. Are you sure you want a husband, or is a room mate what you need?

❖ 5 ❖

HIS WIFE OR
HIS ROOM MATE?

A room mate is a person who shares a residence with you. The most common reason for shared housing is to reduce the cost of housing. Your roomy may also cause you less privacy.

Other motivations for rooming are to gain better amenities than those available in single-person housing (swimming pool, tennis court, walking/biking trail, safer playgrounds, better schools), to share the work of maintaining a household (cleaning, vacuuming, window washing, toilets, shoveling snow) and to have the companionship of other people (at your convenience, of course).

Well sweetness, being a helper to your husband is an up close and personal covenant calling. I urge all my sisters to please, strongly resist the temptation to substitute this sacred role as a helper and suitable companion for your husband just for the opportunity to have someone pay half of your living expenses.

Living with a man does not make you his wife. You can not practice marriage. It is a union originated by God where a man and his wife become one flesh.

A husband is a husband and a room mate is a room mate. Don't get it twisted. Or should I say, don't keep it twisted.

I bet you have thought of a dozen people who should be reading this book. Good. Buy all of them a copy and give or mail it to them.

In this way they can get mad at me instead of you.

So girls, avoid getting married when all you really need is a good room mate. Simply place a classified ad on Craig's List or your local newspaper or put the word out on Facebook.

Girls, we were created to be more than candy for a sugar daddy.

6

SWEET AND LOW
(A SUGAR DADDY)

I define a sugar daddy usually as an older man who provides material things for an woman without any marital covenant agreement. She gets to brag to her friends and he gets to show you off to his friends and use you as he pleases. Girls, a sugar daddy just wants candy.

According to the *American Heritage Dictionary* a sugar daddy is a wealthy, usually older man who gives expensive gifts to a young person in return for sexual favors or companionship.

So, if ching-ching and bling-bling is all you desire, then a sugar daddy may be enough for a while. However, as a woman, I know that deep down in your heart, a sugar daddy or a pimp is not what you really want or need.

May I encourage you again to get to know your real daddy, if possible. Education yourself, get a job/career. Working hard with your own hands allows you to pay for your own manicures, pedicures, hair styling, designer clothes, bags and shoes. Until then, buy yourself affordable gifts. Shop at thrift stores, yard sales, estate sales, church clothes closets. Take yourself to dinner or learn to cook your favorite meals at home.

If you are reading this and you are in a compromising situation that is less than favorable right now, just know this—your Heavenly

Father loves you more than you could ever know and He has wonderful plans for your life. He will never turn away anyone who comes to Him. There is nothing you can do to make Him love you any more or any less than He does right now.

If you need a way out, Father God will provide a way of escape for you. He's supernatural, you know. Nothing is impossible with Him.

Why don't you just pause right now and invite Christ into your life. Ask the Father for the wisdom you need to live the abundant life He has for you.

I join my spirit and my faith to yours and I pray you will open the door of your heart and let Him lead you into a brand new life.

Let me know you prayed this prayer. Remember, I can be reached at wifeschool@verizon.net. Every effort will be made to respond to all e-mails.

Many women, especially single mothers, may simply have to do without some things until we are able to obtain them in a way that bring us joy and inner peace at the end of the day.

I am not judging any one who is in a bad situation. Trust me, I know better. I too have done things I am not proud of to provide for my children. Thank God for grace and mercy.

Ladies, can we talk baby daddy?

◆ 7 ◆

MY BABY DADDY

I need me a man to help me raise my kids with or
without a covenant union of marriage.
—*B. J.'s definition*

The Urban Dictionary defines *baby daddy* as, short for "baby's daddy," the father of your child, whom you did not marry, and with whom you are not currently involved.

Being a wife must be about more than help with your babies/children. Plenty help is out there, there are daycares, pre-school, grandparents, retired family members and friends, Boys and Girls Club, Big Brothers/Big Sisters, church members, good neighbors, need I go on?

A word of caution to all young mothers—please be careful and do your homework when looking for quality help with your children. Your children are a gift from God and you are totally responsible for their care. Please do not allow someone or some thing to cloud your judgment as many women have. Avoid wolves in sheep clothing. When in doubt, seek and receive Godly counsel.

A true wife's purpose is to be a counterpart and helper that is right for him (her husband). Be sure you are not wanting to marry to get revenge with a baby daddy or a ex-husband, or just to get a daddy for your children. Forgiveness is the best revenge, is what I always say.

It is my hope that you are clear on how a wife's role with her husband differs from a father figure, an enabler, a room mate, a sugar daddy or a baby daddy.

Wives, your husband must be a priority even when there are children involved. Are you listening? Are you sure you're listening?

I believe a Godly husband will seek his wife. So ladies you can burn up your "I Will Not Settle For Less" list and stop the man hunt and let him find you. Build you, and he will come.

❖ 8 ❖

I WILL NOT SETTLE!

Precious daughters, I say this with all the love in my heart. You need to close your "Build-A-Husband Shop."

By the way, how's that list working for you? You know that checklist (written or mental) that itemizes all the qualities your man will possess.

You know those things that you said, "I'll be damned if I will settle for any man who...." So you start your "Build-a-Man" list that may look something like this:

- ✓ Tall, dark and don't forget handsome. He must be easy on the eyes. Yes ma'am, I need me a good looking man.

- ✓ He must know how to dress well. One of those suit-wearing, briefcase-carrying, lawyer types will do.

- ✓ My soul mate will be highly educated. He must have a Masters Degree, but a Doctorate will be even better.

✓ A J-O-B? Hell no, not just a J-O-B! He has got to have a real good job with benefits—top salary, good healthcare plan, 401k, retirement/savings plan. He is going to have to take care of me and my children, because I'm sick and tired of doing everything by myself.

✓ He has got to have money, lots of money, and be liberal with it. I can't stand a cheap, stingy man. He must make more money than me or I don't need him. I can do bad all by myself.

✓ Girl, did I say muscles? He better have at least a six pack. No flabby man for me. A gym membership is a must (I like 'em buff and educated).

✓ He must have all of his own pearly white, even teeth. No hearing aides. No limps.

✓ His eyes will be deep and romantic. No cross-eyed man for me, cause I won't be able tell if he is looking at me or some other woman across the room.

✓ I need someone who will love me unconditionally for who I am. He will listen when I talk without judging or criticizing. Someone who will be sensitive to my needs, and will always be there for me, who will have my back for a change.

✓ Lord have mercy, I forgot one of the most important things. Girlfriend, how could you let me forget, SEXY? He has got to be good in bed. I want him to be able to rock my world.

Now the *church girls* list may include everything above and a few more add-ons like:

✓ Must be able to pray at least an hour (in tongues and with understanding).

✓ Read his Bible everyday and know it from cover to cover.

✓ Have regular Bible study in the home with his family.

✓ Help with the household chores .

✓ Plan romantic dinners and get-a-ways without being told.

✓ Go to church every Sunday and whenever the door is open.

✓ Must be a tither and a giver (cause I don't want my family cursed).

✓ He can not have a criminal record. That's right, no jail time. I don't care if the charges were dropped. A copy of his criminal history record required.

✓ He must teach my son how to play ball and change tires and men stuff.

✓ He need to protect my daughter from bad boys and teach her what to look for in a man.

✓ He needs a good mind. He can't be forgetting birthdates and important stuff.

The best advice I can give all Godly women from the Father's heart is tear your list up and burn it (whether written or mental, destroy it). Yep, hit the delete key. Now and go to the recycle bin and delete it permanently. Close your little "Build-a-Man" shop forever.

You can destroy your list because you are not seeking a husband, you unmarried ladies are seeking the Kingdom. Therefore, no list is needed. You need a trusting heart that your husband who is seeking a wife will find you at the time appointed by the Father.

Until then, remember, you are your Heavenly Father's good thing first. Fully submit to this truth. Those who have chosen to live by Heavens rule are no longer living by the traditions of men. Traditions of man make the Word of God ineffective.

God's laws governing the universe regarding wives were here before we were born. He has already written the standard for husband and wives and we have His Spirit to teach and guide us each day. Father knows best and His ways are excellent.

Your man list is a tradition of man. It is something that has been passed down from generation to generation by oral communication and have no true Biblical basis at all.

◆ Suggested Prayer for Unmarried Ladies ◆

Father, You know what is best for me. You made me and know me better than anyone else on earth, and I trust You to help me prepare to a be a wife according to Your Will. You will let me be found in Your timing by the husband of Your dreams. I am Your good thing to the husband You have appointed. I will keep my eyes on You.

Amen.

You see ladies, when you make the list and build your own husband, then you are responsible for the outcome, the plan originated from you. When God does it, then He is obligated to fulfill His Word, and hold everything together by the Word of His Power.

Does a Godly woman really have to tell the Sovereign God that she wants a Godly husband? Or tell the Provider that she needs provision? Or tell Love Himself that she needs love?

As wives, our lives revolve around believing the truth that Father God loves us and He forever has our best interest at heart. Learn to hear the voice of Love inside you speaking and living.

Precious ones, cast down all negative thoughts that if you wait on the Lord, he will make you marry someone you don't like—some old, bald-headed, fat, toothless, potbellied, ugly, jobless, still living with his mama ... man.

Your Daddy loves you, and with all His heart, and wants you to have an abundant life of love, peace and joy. His desire is to do you good and not harm all the days of your life. Own this today.

Simply pray: "Father, these are my innermost fears about being a Godly wife. I give them all to you today. Forgive me for not trusting You as I should. I'm just finding out how good You really are. I will put my trust in You completely. Your ways are excellent!"

Sisters, I trust by now all of your "Build-a-Husband" lists are destroyed and you fully agree it is God's plan for the man to find his wife. Hopefully, you have resolved to be a wife who is devoted to her God and her husband.

I know, I know you are now asking, what do I do with all my free time? Well, I'm glad you asked.

Keep reading, I'm going to help you find something constructive to do while you are preparing and patiently waiting to be found.

❖ 9 ❖

LET HIM FIND YOU

Women of God, while you are waiting to be found, continue to renew your thinking and come into full agreement with God about what it means to be a suitable helper for your husband.

Now here is a possible replacement for your former list:

✓ Study the Word of God, especially what He says about marriage. Meditate and pray the Word.

✓ Become economically empowered. Financial management in marriage is a must. If you can't manage your money, how will you handle your household budget? Do you even know the difference in a want and a need? Purchase your own home if able; if not, take a first-time home buyers class to prepare for home ownership.

✓ Work on your appearance. Practice daily personal hygiene care and good grooming.

✓ Get a quality education if at all possible. Educated men usually like to take home educated women.

✓ Those who are parents, make sure your children are well-mannered. Take parenting classes when needed. Check the internet for free help or watch shows like *Nanny 911*. A lot of churches now offer parenting classes.

✓ Also remember, if you have daughters, chances are you are raising someone's wife (my son, Quentin reminded me to add this last statement). When unsure about your parenting skills, ask someone that you know loves you and will tell you the truth. The truth may offend a little at first.

✓ Practice self-control. If you have anger problems, admit it and get help. Go to anger management classes when needed. Tell yourself the truth. Listen to those who love you.

✓ Develop a hobby/trade. Even when married you need something that you enjoy doing with your hands. It is great therapy. God often speaks to me when I'm sewing or cooking or reading.

✓ Learn to prepare basic meals (more on this topic later).

✓ Learn basic sewing skills (hemming, sewing on buttons, repairing torn seams). This one skill has saved me lots of money on seamstress bills and from throwing away good clothes due to minor repairs needed.

✓ Learn to talk less to others and more to the Father. Study to be quiet. Men usually don't use as many words as women. This discipline is highly needful in being a wife. Most women talk too much.

✓ Fall in love with God. You were created to love and be loved by Him first.

✓ Mature in your spiritual fruit and gifts. Know and fulfill your spiritual purpose.

✓ Mentor/tutor a child. Volunteer at your local church or a community event. I believe everyone should have a mentor and be a mentor.

✓ Become a foster parent. Open your heart and home to a child who has been abused or neglected and is need of some love, patience and understanding.

✓ Get to know and love yourself, the beautiful woman inside you and the little girl inside. Enjoy being alone. FYI, you are never alone. You may feel lonely at times, but you are never alone. Feelings are feelings. Truth is Truth. God is Spirit. He's always with you. He never sleeps. Daily allow Father to download revelation of His love in you.

I could go on and on, but you get the picture. Don't over extend yourself with too many things at once. Father is always first, then choose a goal and put your heart and soul into it. Once it is accomplished, reward yourself and continue.

Unmarried women, let him find you being:

A diligent seeker of spiritual Truth
A doer of good works (in your home, church, community)
A lover of God, others and yourself (in word and deed)
Caring for the unfortunate (orphans, widows, sick, elderly, incarcerated)

Mentoring/tutoring a pupil
Honoring your parents, leaders and country
A faithful, dependent, loyal employee/employer
Honest, trustworthy, kind, sweet, humble
A Soul-winner, freely sharing your faith
A devoted worshipper of God
A diligent user of your gifts and talents
Filled with and led by the Spirit of Truth
Loving just like your Heavenly Father (being a daddy's girl)

Ladies I truly believe if you will build you, he will come. Promise yourself you will stop worrying about the who, when and where. Concentrate on and enjoy your life here and now. See every day as a gift from God. Do your best to enjoy the people that are in your life today.

Who knows, he (your husband) may already be watching you. Okay, that's enough about letting him find you.

FYI, if you are a Pastor or Women's Leader or would like to host a small or large Wife School conference in your area, please feel free to contact me at wifeschool@verizon.net, and put Wife School Conference in the subject line. My heart's desire is to help the women of the world become the wives of Father's dreams.

Now, how many of you know the difference between a wedding planner and a wife? Believe me when I tell you from my experience as marriage prep facilitator, many women think having a wedding makes them a wife. This next chapter is not for the faint of heart, only for those who can handle raw, real, radical truth. Trust me when I tell you this book and ministry is needful. Don't you dare throw this book in the trash—keep reading girlfriends, keep reading. You might just learn something.

◆ 10 ◆

A WIFE OR A WEDDING PLANNER (REMEMBER, YOU WERE WARNED)

It never ceases to amaze me how much time, energy and money some women are willing to use, spend and invest preparing for a wedding, "their special day." Many are trying to live out some childhood Cinderella fantasy. Yet, most will spend little to no time or money preparing to be a wonderful wife to her husband, and acquiring the skills needed for parenting.

Countless women spend years of their lives and multiple thousands of dollars educating themselves for jobs, careers, trades, and hobbies. Yet many of these same women fail to invest in educating and preparing for one of the most important roles they will ever function in on earth. A wife.

Any female can be a bride for a day, and impress her family and friends. Been there, done that twice. But only a wife is ready, willing and able to embrace the selfless day-to-day life of being a helper from God suitable for her husband. Please renew your mind baby girl.

If I were you, I would give a copy of this book as a gift at all bridal/wedding showers, to anyone considering getting married, recently married or those who are married and could benefit from a few reminders of what God intended a wife to be.

If you equate being a wife as simply receiving a huge diamond, wearing a beautiful white designer gown, having a big reception and a spending a dream honeymoon on a fantasy island, please think again. If this is your perception of what constitutes a wife, might I suggest, just stop by a local jewelry store in your city, buy yourself a birthstone or a nice tennis bracelet. A wedding ring symbolizes an unending covenant commitment to be a helper suitable to your husband. If white is your color, simple purchase yourself some beautiful white designer outfits. Throw yourself a birthday party and invite your friends. In lieu of a honeymoon, take one of those $299 Bahamas cruises with a friend or two.

If you are captivated by weddings, maybe you should consider becoming a wedding planner.

Many women (and men) marry without ever familiarizing themselves with the basic traditional wedding vows. Some don't remember what they vowed to on their wedding day until they watch the video. You know those vows that state something like this:

> I promise before God and these witnesses
> To be your wedded wife
> To have and to hold
> From this day forward
> For better, for worst
> For richer, for poorer
> In sickness and in health
> Until death parts us.

I do realize that I could get killed by some religious communities for this next question, but here it is! Are wedding vows even Biblical? Inquiring minds want to know. If you know the answer to this, do enlighten me at wifeschool@verizon.net. I don't profess to have all the answers on this subject or any subject. If I am not mistaken, I thought I read somewhere not to make any vows at all, to let your yes be yes, and your no be no, and that anything beyond that is of evil. Yes, I went there.

Let's suppose this is the case. Then in my opinion, the needful things at a wedding ceremony is ministry (prayer/blessings) for the couple and they agree with a yes or no to take each other as spouses. I am B. J. Fountain, and for now this is my take on this subject. To vow or not to vow, this is the question. Holla!

I am now married over twenty years to the man I know God sent to find me.

I would love to share more on how Wil and I met, and how I knew I was his helper sent from God. Yes ladies, you can know beyond a reasonable doubt whether or not you are his wife.

Can you stand a little more raw truth? It's for your own good, you'll see. I want you all to be wise women, not foolish.

❖ 11 ❖

DON'T BE FOOLED

Okay, Miss Attitude, hold on to your seat and remain teachable. Marriage is a God idea.

You cannot turn a fool into a husband. No amount of munipulation through kinky sex, home cooked meals, money loans, free housing, expensive jewelry and gifts, domestic services, pretty babies, or even long prayers can accomplish this task. Here's the proof:

> The fool has said in his heart, "There is no God."
> —Psalm 53:1

> A fool has no delight in understanding, but in expressing his own heart.
> —Proverbs 18:2

> He who trusts in his own heart is a fool....
> —Proverbs 28:26

> The way of a fool is right in his own eyes, but he who heeds counsel is wise.
> —Proverbs 12:15

He who walks with wise men will be wise, but the companion of fools will be destroyed.

—Proverbs 13:20

Now we have received, not the spirit of the world, but the spirit which is of God; that we might know the things that are freely given to us of God.

—1 Corinthians 2:12

The unmarried wife knows within herself that she is her husband's good thing, and that it's only a matter of time before he finds her.

She is patient in her wait. She has ceased ALL fussing, fuming, worrying and grieving about the who and when, and she is enjoying life one day at a time.

She is preparing herself spiritually, physically, emotionally and financially to be a helper to her spouse.

◆ 12 ◆

SPIRIT, SOUL AND BODY

For all wives and wives to be, you must be strong in spirit, having fully embraced deep inner healing, physically up for the challenge, and financially wise to be a wife.

◆ Strong in Spirit ◆

Your spirit will grow strong from trusting God and His Word regarding being found of her husband.

> Trust in the LORD with all your heart and lean not on
> your own understanding; in all your ways submit to
> Him, and He will make your paths straight.
> —Proverbs 3:5-6 (NIV)

◆ Healing for the Soul ◆

Wise women have freed themselves of all known baggage from prior toxic relationships by asking and receiving, from Father alone, healing for her broken heart (from loss, death, divorce, betrayal, rejection, sexual abuse) and the binding up of all wounds from every unhealthy soul ties.

> He is the healer of the brokenhearted. He is the one
> who bandages their wounds.
> —Psalms 147:3

> The LORD is close to the brokenhearted; he rescues
> those whose spirits are crushed.
> —Psalms 34:18

◈ Care for Her Body ◈

A true wife loves her own body before expecting her husband to love it. Don't like what you see in the mirror? What are you going to do about it? How will you take care of your husband and family if you are unhappy and unhealthy? It's your body. Love it or begin the process of changing it (healthier diet, exercise, get rid of stress).

Some wise advice to unmarried wives, don't be afraid to visit a medical doctor with your fiance. Make sure he is in fact, a "he." Protect yourself and your spouse from sexually transmitted disease. It's never too early to be honest. Remember, if you have received Christ, the Spirit of Truth lives in you. Some truths to ponder:

> I praise You because I am fearfully and wonderfully
> made; Your works are wonderful, I know that full
> well.
> —Psalm 139:14

What? Know ye not that your body is the temple of
the Holy Ghost which is in you, which ye have of
God, and ye are not your own?
—I Cor 6:19

The wife hath not power of her own body, but the
husband: and likewise also the husband hath not
power of his own body, but the wife.
—I Cor 7:4

◆ Financially Prudent ◆

A real wife handles her finances well and looks forward to helping
her husband manage their household affairs. She knows how to earn,
save, give and invest money.

No one can serve two masters. Either you will hate
the one and love the other, or you will be devoted to
the one and despise the other. You cannot serve both
God and money.
—Matt 6:24

The wise woman builds her house, but with her own
hands the foolish one tears hers down.
—Proverbs 14:1

Houses and wealth are inherited from parents, but a
prudent wife is from the LORD.
—Proverbs 19:14

> A wife of noble character who can find? She is worth
> far more than rubies. Her husband has full confidence
> in her and lacks nothing of value. She brings him
> good, not harm, all the days of her life.
>
> —Proverbs 31:10-12

Ladies, even if your husband handles all the household finances, you should be aware of all money matters in your home. Be prepared in case of an unexpected accident, sickness or death, so you will be able to manage things in his absence. You need to know about all mortgages, bank accounts, medical and life insurance, investments, auto loans, credit card debt.

Discuss what his wishes are in the event he becomes disabled or in case of some unforeseen event. Find out where the important personal documents are kept, including a will, life insurance policies, auto policies, mortgage deeds, etc.

Most wives fear this subject—death. Wil and I have discussed both of our deaths seriously and jokingly. It's important to know each other's wishes and how each feels about death itself. We both have written wills. We both want to be cremated and we both are organ donors.

See, that's not hard. Deal with it once and for all and keep enjoying life.

• 13 •

WHAT A REAL WIFE KNOWS

A real wife is a whole woman (spirit, soul, body). She is no longer seeking outside of herself for that which can only be found within. No other person, place or thing could make her more complete. She knows the true source of her being and is at one with herself and her Creator.

A true wife can confidently define herself, which is ever changing, and her worldview to her husband and to the world. I believe every Godly woman (devoted to God, His Word, His Will), has the potential to be a great wife. We are our Father's daughters. There is greatness in all of us, so many worlds (dimensions) just waiting to be discovered.

A true wife loves her God, herself, her family, her friends and her world.

The real wife is continually getting to know her Heavenly Father and her husband. She began this process long before her wedding day. Each day she lives to love and be loved, to give and to forgive.

She knows her husband is human and will always have faults, and at the same time she realizes she is his suitable helper sent from God. She knows her husband's spirit. She always goes to Father first for all issues regarding him (not family or friends). She prays daily for him no matter what she is feeling. All problems with her husband are resolved in a Godly manner (as quickly and as respectfully as possible).

The true wife understands the needs of her husband. When she is unsure she is not afraid to ask him. Those needs may include sex, food, car, sports, TV, tools, hobbies, friends, love and respect from his wife.

❖ 14 ❖

WHAT A HUSBAND WANTS
AND NEEDS

❖ Great Sex ❖

It's okay to ask your spouse, "How may I be more pleasing to you sexually? How am I doing as your wife? What will make me a better helper for you?"

A real wife knows that sexual intimacy is a God idea for husbands and wives to privately enjoy in any manner they deem pleasurable and that they both agree upon. Remember beloved, men didn't invent sex. God is the originator of sex and every other good thing.

Meeting her husband's sexual needs in the bedroom (or any location agreed upon) is a wife's responsibility alone. No other woman on earth has the legal or God-given right or is entitled to this privilege. A real wife considers it an honor to please and to be pleasured by her husband sexually.

My advice to Godly married women is, "When at all possible, NEVER SAY NO" to sexual intimacy with your husband.

I believe love will find a way. Wives, making love can always be a joyful win-win situation. You must resolve to make every effort to give him what he needs, how he needs it and when he needs it. There are many resources available to help you in this area. Contact me if you need referrals.

Unless you are severely ill, lame excuses are not acceptable reasons for refusing to meet your husband's sexual needs. Girls you know what I am talking about. "I'm too tired." "I don't feel like it." "I have a headache." "I'm just not in the mood." "All you men think about is sex, sex, sex."

Ladies, how many other things do we wives do throughout the day even when we are tired? We work at our jobs tired, go shopping tired, take care of the children tired, go to church tired. Why is it that we can do mostly anything else while tired, but feel we have to draw the line when it comes to the one we have vowed to love and cherish forever? Hope you are being enlightened.

I know some of the religious community will not like this, but I'm okay with that. As a minister I will do all I can to help the women of God enjoy their sexuality and love every facet of being a wife.

Trust me, everything that I am teaching you, I also practice faithfully in my own marriage. Remember, I grew up in a generation that did not discuss sex in the home and definitely not at church. All that I learned about sex came from the street through perverted people, dirty magazines, and the internet. None of the Godly women in my life taught me how to be a pleasing sexual partner to my husband. The Christians I grew up around seemed to view sex as nasty or something to be tolerated by women in marriage. During my youth I never heard a married woman say she enjoyed sex with her husband.

One of the older teen girls in the neighborhood taught me and other young girls how to masturbate. I grew up literally fighting with boys and grown men to keep my virginity (including cousins and uncles).

Precious wives, marriage is until death part us. A wife must keep learning new ways to satisfy her spouse. True wives are not intimidated to initiate sexual intimacy and can communicate her needs to her husband.

There was a time when I dreaded sexual intimacy, until I got a revelation of God's love for me. He desires that I enjoy life—every part of my life. I began to understand that my husband not only loves having sex with me, he loves me. So I prayed, "Okay God, about this sex thing. I want to love it and enjoy it as much as he does." I told my husband what I had prayed. I bought books and began to learn new sex positions and techniques. I fellowship with Godly women who love their husbands and who encourage me to please my husband. Ladies, married life is too long to be miserably enduring sex. Love it or get help today. Let me know if I can help.

All known sexual problems should be dealt with before marriage, when possible. Marriage is not a cure-all for sexual addictions and other immoral behavior. Your husband needs to know if you have been raped and abused in any way. He is not a mind reader. Talk openly and honestly to him and pray together about issues of importance.

Put all pride aside and seek professional help when needed. There are lots of resources available to help you keep sexual intimacy enjoyable for you and your husband.

We discuss this and more in detail at Wife School. Hope to see you at a gathering in your area. Until we meet, you may direct any questions or comments to me at wifeschool@verizon.net.

◆ Good Food ◆

Sisters, you must plan on making sure your husband is fed well. I realize some households prefer personal cooks. I ain't mad, but this is not so of the average household.

If you can read, you can cook. Can you say "Food Network?"

Just pick one—Paula Deene, B. Smith, G. Garvin, Rachel Ray. There are thousands of free recipes on the internet as well. While you are on Facebook, put your face in a cook book.

Unless you and your spouse have made other arrangements, my advice is every wife should know how to prepare basic meals before marriage. Learn to make your spouse's favorite meals at home. Kindly and gradually introduce new foods to your husband. Respect any cultural difference.

It may be necessary to learn to make his mama's rolls or his grandmother's sweet potato pies. Use this as an opportunity to bond with his family.

A wise wife knows how to keep her husband home for meals, whether, from a slow cooker, a candlelight meal with china, delivery pizza or picking up Chinese. Practice makes perfect. Keep trying until you get it right. He'll love you for it.

Cook smarter, not harder—prepare several meals at once. Planning is essential. Lots of meals are precooked or fully prepared these days.

FYI, mothers with sons, remember this: you are raising another woman's husband. Teach your sons to cook and basic housekeeping skills. Your daughter-in-law will love you like mine does.

❂ A Sweet Ride ❂

Girls, you do know by now that there is something special between a man and his vehicles. You may never understand it, but he does. You don't have to understand it, just respect him and his automobile.

There is something about a man and engines. Wives, if your budget can afford the car your husband wants, get it for him. If not, pray, save and budget until he can get it. Let him know it is important to you that he has the car of his choice. Since God is doing the providing, it's no harder to believe for two cars (one for you).

◆ Large Screen TV ◆

Oh, yeah! This is a necessity for most men. His needs his own flat screen with a remote control. Chances are he likes some kind of sport. He will usually have his favorite football team. My husband likes the Chicago Bears. Never, I say, *never* interfere with him enjoying his favorite shows and games. Quietly, join him or spend that time enjoying you.

◆ Tools ◆

Not every husband is a "Mr. Fix-it," but most will need at least a small tool set. Encourage any and all attempts to repair anything in or around the home. With HGTV, it is not uncommon these days that the wife is the fix-it person around the house. If so, know that you are still being his helper from God. It is unwise to belittle him privately or publicly for his lack of skills in any area. Wives, you are to help him, and never criticize him.

◆ A Hobby ◆

Every husband needs to have something he enjoys doing and is passionate about. Encourage your husband in his hobby. My husband, Wil, is passionate about fishing. I listen to all his fish stories. Sometimes I go fishing with him, not because I love fishing, but because I love him. I call to check on him when he goes fishing alone or with friends. I ask him the same two questions each time, "Have you caught dinner yet?" and "Are you having fun?" His usual response is to laugh and to say "yes" to both questions, unless he is catching a fish at the time I call, then he says "Babe can't talk to you now, call me back."

◆ A Supportive Spouse ◆

Encourage, edify and build up your husband continually. Compliment him often. Thank him for everything he does for you, your children or around the house. Simply, kiss him and say, "Honey thank you for washing the car, I appreciate you." Keep an atmosphere of peace in your home.

Maintain a beautiful, clean house. Clean it yourself or have it cleaned professionally. Just remember—the clean up woman is a woman too. If you have children, teach them household responsibility. Treat your husband with respect and he will help with the house cleaning. I am blessed to have a husband who does 95% of the household cleaning. Not bragging, I have been favored by God and this same favor is yours.

Support your husband in all his efforts and endeavors (legal efforts, that is).

He may have tried and failed at a business or two. Still pray for and with him. Encourage him to try again. Many famous people failed several times before they were successful.

With unemployment at an all time high, your husband may be out of work. You are his helper, don't turn on him when he is down. He really needs his wife's support. Honor him and hold him up in prayer until he is employed again. It is never okay to demean your spouse or any other creation of God. If not you, then who?

Encourage him regarding his health and well being. Sweetly remind him to get an annual physical, dental, eye exam. Help him by making his appointments and accompany him when able. If you notice a change, try saying, "I notice you seem tired a lot lately, would you like me to pick you up some vitamins while I'm out?" "You seem irritable, have you eaten and taken your meds?" "You've been working on the car a long time, I'm fixing some ice tea, why don't you come in and rest for a few minutes?"

You can help your husband by simply noticing when he's not himself. This can be done without nagging or judging. "Babe, are you okay? You don't seem like yourself today. Is there something I can help you with?" Ladies, this is what a husband needs and wants.

Ladies, embrace your husband's friends and family. A wise woman respects her husband's choice of friends. She receives his friends as hers, and his family has now become her family. Pray for them and build healthy relationships when possible.

There must be scheduled time for you and your spouse alone. Plan creative, affordable things you both can enjoy doing together. It doesn't matter who plans the event, just enjoy being together.

❖ 15 ❖

LITTLE THINGS

I want to thank you so much for reading my first book. I'm already getting ideas and suggestions for the next one. I trust you have been enlightened in your role as a Godly wife. Please pass it on to another woman who can benefit from its wisdom treasures.

In this final chapter I want to teach you wise women some simple things that will help you become an extraordinary wife.

❖ Say Good Morning ❖

Greet your husband in the morning, afternoon or evening with eye contact and touch when possible. Kiss him before he leaves for work and wish him a great day.

❖ Please and Thank You ❖

We use manners with everyone else. Your husband deserves no less. Don't take him for granted.

◆ Check on Him ◆

It only takes a minute to call and see how his day is going. It has never been easier to communicate than it is today. Text him, fax him, e-mail him, Facebook him. Just let him know you are thinking of him.

◆ Say "I Love You" ◆

Tell your husband you love him daily. Tell him what you love about him often.

◆ Enjoy Sexual Intimacy ◆

Never say no to sexual intimacy with your spouse. Don't be ashamed to initiate love making and to try new methods. Be open to pleasure enhancers. If you don't love having sex with your husband, there is a problem. Seek help. Husbands love sex. Marriage is for life, so sexual intimacy with him is for life. Forgive me for being redundant. Sex—love it or get help today.

◆ Accept His Family ◆

Pursue peace with your in-laws. Never badmouth them to your husband. Pray, state the facts, forgive and keep moving forward. Your husband should never have to choose between his family and his wife. Disagreements are inevitable in any relationship. When possible, the wife should deal with conflicts involving her family, and the husband should deal with his family's issues.

◆ Dream Together ◆

Never compete with your husband. You are one flesh. When you love him, you are loving yourself. When he succeeds, you succeed. As you submit your heart to him, he will submit his heart to you.

◆ Pray Daily ◆

Pray for your husband everyday, even when you don't feel like it. Pray about everything that concerns him. Never involve family members or friends in your personal marriage affairs. Discuss your husband's faults with him and God alone. Forgive his faults, shortcomings and offenses quickly and thoroughly.

◆ Be Sweet ◆

Wives of the world, there is nothing more beautiful than a woman with a sweet, calm spirit. Being an extraordinary wife will not happen overnight. It will require renewing of the mind. It will involve constant effort on your part, until it becomes natural. Your husband is going to love his new wife.

◆ Always Remember ◆

Marriage is a God idea. God joined you both together. You are his *good thing*—his suitable, compatible helper from God. Your husband has favor with God because of you. What God has joined together, let no man separate.

God bless you.

◆ ABOUT THE AUTHOR ◆

Dr. B. J. Fountain is the founder of Wife School and Beauty for Ashes Ministries, Inc. B. J. and her husband, Wil are Senior Pastors of Kingdom Living Fellowship Int'l, Inc. in Richmond, VA. She is an author, international speaker, and an anointed praise and worship leader. B. J. is devoted to God, her family, and the ministry of the Kingdom of God. She is presently being used mightily by the Lord to train women of faith to be extraordinary wives.

> **For a Wife School Conference or Seminar at your church, organization or women's group, please contact me at wifeschool@verizon.net.**